Usborne
Words

At the back of this book, you'll find instructions for **two matching games** to play with the **cards** and **boards** in this pack. They're a great way for children to learn to **recognize and read simple words.**

ant

apple

bell

bird

bus

cat

cheese

cherry

clock

crab

dog

drum

duck

fish

flag

fox

frog

hat

hen

king

leaf

parrot

pen

queen

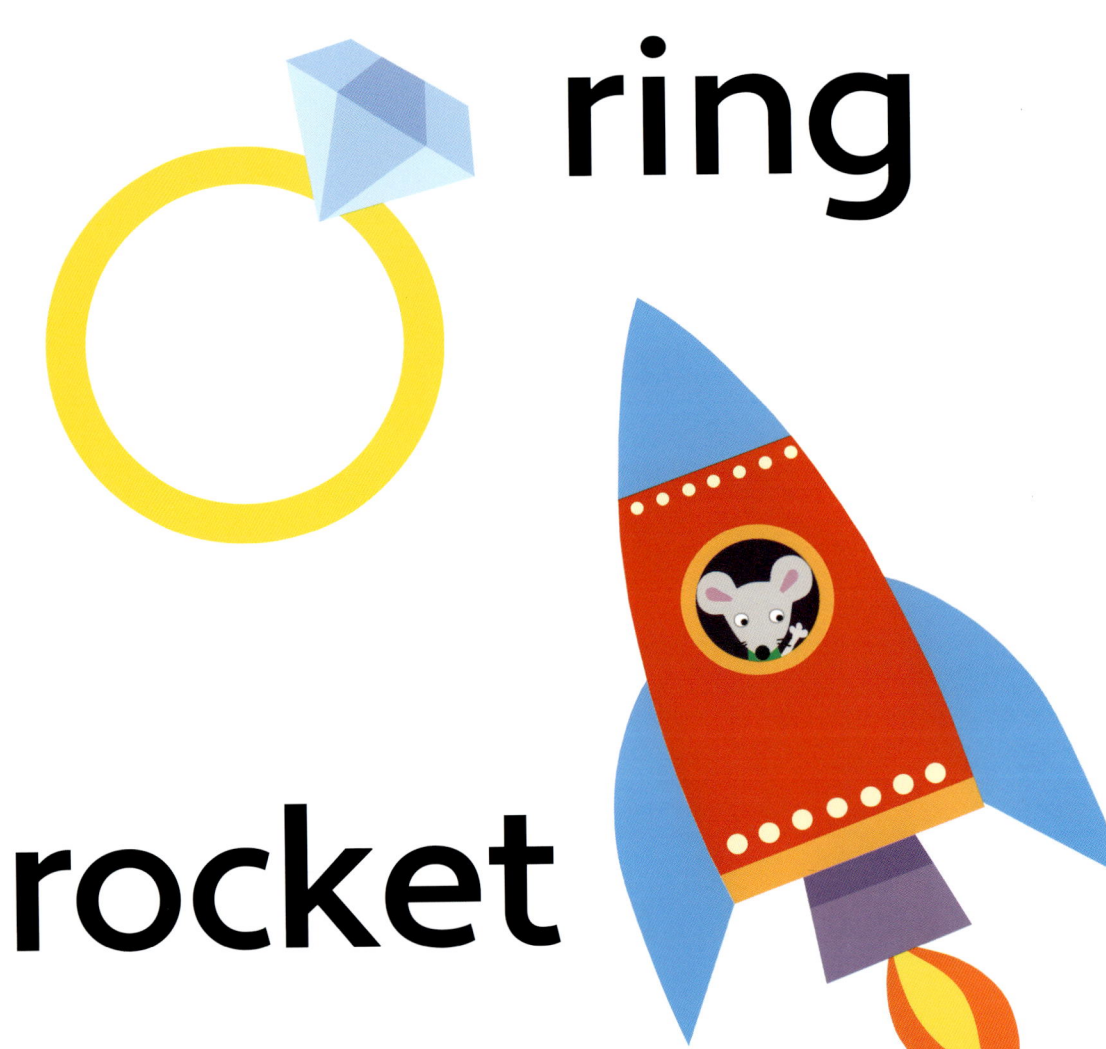

ring

rocket

shark

sheep

ship

socks

sun

tree

truck

van

witch

zebra

How to play words memory game

In this game for 2, 3 or 4 players, children need to look at the cards carefully and remember where they are, developing observation and memory skills.

1. Each player takes a board:

hat	truck	bell
bird	crab	witch
dog	sun	cherry

cat	ship	hen
frog	cheese	fish
clock	tree	bus

apple	parrot	ring
fox	drum	rocket
van	shark	queen

sheep	pen	flag
duck	king	zebra
socks	leaf	ant

2. Mix up the cards and lay them all out, face down.

3. Take turns to choose a card and turn it over.

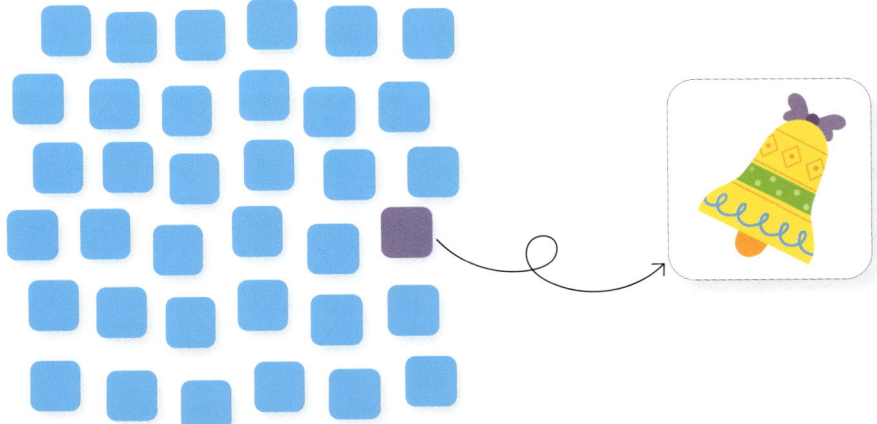

4. If the picture on the card matches a word on your board, put the card on top.

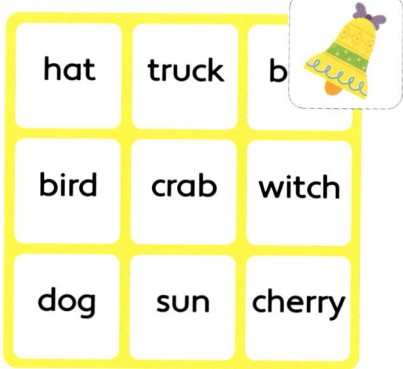

hat	truck	b
bird	crab	witch
dog	sun	cherry

b e l l
spells **bell**!
I need this card.

5. If you don't need the card, put it back where you found it, face down. Then it's the next player's turn.

The word "tree" isn't on my board.

6. You win by being the first to fill your board.

Top tip: when another player turns over a card you need, remember where it is so you can pick it up on your next turn.

How to play words bingo

This game can be played with 2, 3, 4 or 5 players. It's ideal for developing speaking and listening skills as children talk about the cards they need.

1. One person mixes up all the cards, keeping them face down. That person is the caller. Everyone else takes a board:

hat	truck	bell
bird	crab	witch
dog	sun	cherry

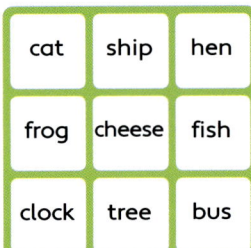

cat	ship	hen
frog	cheese	fish
clock	tree	bus

apple	parrot	ring
fox	drum	rocket
van	shark	queen

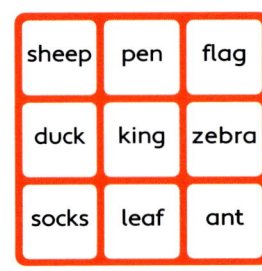

sheep	pen	flag
duck	king	zebra
socks	leaf	ant

2. The caller picks up a card and tells the others what's on it.

It's a cat!

(If there aren't enough players to have a caller, players can take turns to pick up cards and say what's on them.)

3. If the picture on the card matches a word on someone's board, that player takes the card and puts it on top of the word.

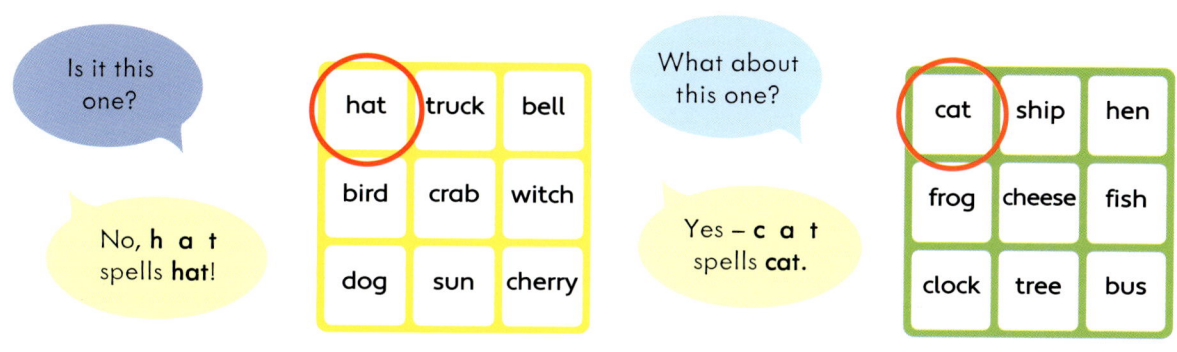

4. If no one needs the card, put it to one side.

5. Keep going until one player's board is complete. That player is the winner, and has to shout "Bingo!"

Written by Kate Nolan
Illustrated by Jayne Schofield
Designed by Jenny Brown

24